YOUR HEART IS THE SEA

Nikita Gill

THOUGHT
CATALOG
Books

Published by Thought Catalog Books, a publishing house owned by The Thought & Expression Company. Art direction by Josh Covarrubias, KJ Parish, and Chris Lavergne. Illustration by Mariana Rodrigues. Printed in 2018. First Edition.

ISBN 978-1-949759-02-0

10 9 8 7 6 5 4 3 2

For you,
and all the darkness
you are holding within you.
This is the place
where you let the light in.

Devour this hungry thing slowly.
Fiction does not live here.
Only a soft true beast they call poetry.

Take this as your warning,
This book will pick out the bones
within you as it picked out the bones
within me.

We are the closets
we hold our skeletons in.
And now they are knocking,
asking to get out.

A REMINDER
BEFORE YOU READ THIS

The first time you hold the disintegrated scaffolding
of the person you used to be, I need you to remember
something they do not teach you in school.

People aren't buildings. We aren't ancient monuments
that, once ravaged by some forgotten war,
lie in permanent ruins of ourselves.

We are made to resolve ourselves.
Paint over the tragedies meant to finish us off in
hues of vibrant pinks and amber and azure skies,

remind ourselves that grief may feel longer
and more poignant than happiness
but it still has an ending.

We house both masterpiece and artist in this skin.
So when you are disintegrated, trying to piece together
what is left inside you, focus on this:

You are not broken.
You are simply disassembled for a while
as the artist inside rebuilds something infinite out of you.

THE ANGUISH

THE DESCENT

YOUR HEART

THE BEGINNING

THE WONDER

THE ACCEPTANCE

THE DEFIANCE

IS THE SEA

THE SURVIVAL

THE WORSHIP

THE
ANGUISH

I learned to make poems
out of the people that burned
and turned me to embers,
the distorted tales
that no one wants to hear.
All this pain
that muffled my screams,
that made me believe
my body–mind–soul was
not mine to keep,
not this way
all ripped up
like the storm
rips the clouds apart
to happen to the earth.
Just to cope.
I did all of this to cope.

I made poems out of the things
that tried to eat my body–mind–soul.

Now I ask you.

What do you do in the dark
when the monsters come for you?

WHY WE ARE ALL AFRAID TO BE

She speaks to me fondly
of passions and talents,
of guitars and stars,
with such breathless intensity
then stops short and
apologizes, ashen-faced
for speaking at all.

All because somewhere in her life,
someone she loved broke her heart
by lashing out with ignorance
at her sublime and pure words
and telling her to
be quiet, stop talking,
because nobody cares.

If you pay attention long enough,
it's a familiar story.
The boy who rarely participates.
The old woman who is too hesitant
to join in a conversation.
The man who thinks three seconds
too long before he speaks.

People aren't born sad.
We make them that way.

THE PAINFUL TRUTH

It is not enough that
they turn you inside out;
they must make
a spectacle out of you.
Those who hurt you
will paint you
with cruel brush strokes,
demonize your goodness
falsify your kindness
vilify your decency.
All this continued harm,
just to justify
their own cruelty
for how brutally
they have
treated you.

BRÛLER

Do not fall in love with me.
Not like this. Not this way.
So wanton and wanting.
So private yet taunting.
You do not know my mind
is a labyrinth of darker things.
There is sin in the science
of how you look at me
and I do not know how to disagree.
You play with my tightly coiled thoughts
like I am nothing and everything at once.
Do not do this. I hid away from you
for a reason. I cannot be one
with this foreboding, intense love.
You have shaken the cage I hold
myself in and for your own good,
heed this warning: Loving me will
be a defiant political quandary.
A shout in the dark.
A way to rebel.
I am the incarnate
of some unfinished thing
and this will be us, too.
So do not come here, brazen,
looking to hold a breathless lover
when I am a calamity.

I am where love goes to die.
And I do not want to do that to you.
I will never be your convenient belief.
So do not trust your love inside
this pit of a human being,
I am an abyss
both cathedral and poison,
and I do not know what I would do
if yet another person I love lost
themselves inside the depths of me.
I do not know if this body can hold
the ends of any more loves, you see.

I NAMED US GRIEF

I called us part dread, part song,
part story, part wrong.

We built castles in each other
out of splintered spine and blood.

We met in grief and
were held together by its mud.

Took crowns made of bones
placed it on each other's heads.

We loved each other with
fragments of ourselves that were dead.

That is why we couldn't rely
on the promises that we spoke.

Perhaps in a different time
I would have named us hope.

Perhaps in a different universe
we would not meet so battle-worn.

And I would call us forgiveness,
and not remember us as war.

A PHILOSOPHICAL QUESTION

Tell me,
if a person falls apart
alone in the dark,
does it make a sound?

And if it does make a sound,
is it as loud and devastating
as a decaying broken heart
when it is finally found?

Or is the sound
a soft strangulation hidden
that we miss all the time
behind words like "I'm fine?"

PROMISES

This is what I have learned about promises:
They are as reliable as false prophets from circuses.

You say to a person who is barely holding it together,
Hold on, I promise, things will get better.

We say, put enough days between the crisis and you,
I promise, time is a great healer of all wounds.

"I promise," however, is only a rope.
It is not and will never be the rescue that we hope.

THE GARDEN

I am unaware when the recovery began
to sound like mutilated mantras
nor when the seeds refused to take root.

Perhaps it was when other people
began to ask me how I was but really meant
"Aren't you over this now, it has been years."

As if healing is a fever that can be measured
by someone else's thermometer.
As if there is a time limit on your trauma and tears.

I read somewhere the other day
that gardening is an act of patience,
because patience is the only way things learn to grow.

So I rake the soil of my mind-earth again,
seeking a softer, more fertile ground
a better place for the healing to flower, to know.

THE CHURCH

My mother told me once
that the only place you
can show those tears,
this grief, be truly vulnerable
is a place of worship.

I do not know how to tell her
when my heart breaks
this body turns into a cathedral,
my eyes turn into fonts,
holy water falling from them
it does not matter where I am,
God takes my hand,
holds my spirit
between his fingers
allows me to let these tears go.

APATHY

The trouble is, you have become too used
to terrible things happening to you.

You learned how to travel through hell
because hell feels like all you ever knew.

The darkness is never a surprise.
The shadows never a shock.

Like a being used to surviving
avalanche after avalanche of rocks.

You carry your pain
like you expect it, and it is no secret.

The bad things, they keep happening.
And you simply sigh and say, "I'm used to it."

A GHOST CALLED DEPRESSION

I crave loneliness so much
I do not want it at all.
Wanting someone's touch
whilst not wanting any other soul.
Needing another voice to say my name
whilst cringing when I am actually called.
There is an empty attic in my head
with a secret chasm where I fall.

So this is what being a ghost feels like
transparent to all except to yourself
you are as real as a city on fire
screaming in burning pain
to a living haunted house
where if the living ever hear you
they think you're a liar.

THE WAR CALLED ANXIETY

Seven years ago,
someone asked me to describe
my anxiety to them and all I could say was
"It is the habit of fashioning bullets
within my head. It is the unwanted practice
of treating my body like it is a pistol,
constantly waiting for someone
to pull my trigger."

If I had any other way to describe this
it would simply be self-defense mode,
like my mind constantly thinks
I am in a bar fight,
in a battlefield,
on top of a building,
and it does everything it can to protect me,
the trouble is, it hasn't learned

the difference between protection
and self-destruction,
and the panic attacks

resemble the soldiers
in the Battle of Karansebes
who accidentally
opened fire on their own
and destroyed their own army.

To the people who have seen me harm
myself, who have watched me fight
and lose against myself,
over and over again
and asked me, "Why do you do this to yourself?,"
all I can say is,
if I knew how to stop this,
if I knew how to do anything
other than simply survive.

Don't you think I would have done it
a long time ago?

LOVER OR PREY

Wolves mate for life.
So do barn owls and eagles.
All of these are predators.

Predators love the same way
they hunt. Violently, powerfully
with razor-sharp precision.

Love can be weaponized.
Love can be dangerous.
What I am trying to say is:

I have been wanted
as much as I have
been hunted.

The trouble is
I cannot tell them
apart anymore.

PAIN IS NO LOVE STORY

Don't let them lie to you and tell you
that pain is romantic or pretty.

Pain is a cemetery of everything
that once made you happy,
everything that you once relied on,
people who promised never to betray you,
relationships painted with forevers
that would never ever come true.

Maybe in songs and in books
people will tell you that it is.

But millions of people kill themselves
every single year
because of all the pain
that they are in
and become statistics,
a testament to how ugly it is.

You are still here for a reason.
And the reason is not to fall in love with your pain.

VULNERABILITY

I still do not know
how to love anyone
who won't show their softest side to me.

And maybe that makes me a monster,
but how can I trust someone
without seeing their vulnerability?

HUNGER

You are a hunger.
A moment left pristine
in the time map of my mind.

I have already baptized
your loss in the salt water
of my tears.

Thought this would
make me forget you,
for you were never a feast,

you were just a craving
that never ever
sated me.

I have talked myself
out of you in every way
I know how.

Found a different love
to feed my love,
yet they tasted bland.

You were
a flavor of ache
and fullness.

And for a while
I have been able to forget
this gnawing

at the pit of
my heart-stomach
for you.

Still, at night,
the darkness comes for me.
Still at night I hunger.

And yet I know
I am hungry
for something that does not exist.

Hungry
for something
we will never be.

HOW TO REMIND YOURSELF YOU EXIST WHEN THE WORLD SAYS YOU DO NOT

1. Get up and wash your face,
the water has always known how to touch your skin
in a way to remind you how real you are.

2. Go to the window. Feel the sun through the filaments
in your hair. Hold the light close to your body.
Let it fill you up.

3. Count your scars, one by one,
but instead of scars, think of them
as journeys that you have taken to become.

4. Allow the pain to come through.
In waves. In whole oceans.
Do not be afraid of it.

5. Turn it into art. Turn it into music.
Carve something beautiful and let it loose
into the world, watch it dance.

6. When all else fails:
Just breathe.
Just breathe.
Just breathe.

AM I THERE YET?

People ask me if the grief has left yet,
a question I ask myself every night
and I always say the same thing,

"Not yet, but then again,
I am here, am I not?
I am smiling. I am holding myself up

despite every stage of terror
grief is putting me through.
I may be living in a house of cards

that its dark hands built
but I am trying to stop myself
from befriending it,

from turning it into a home
and for now this is good enough,
for me, this is good enough."

And they are always taken aback
before they say, "Do you think
recovery is possible from great loss?"

I smile now, hold this broken body
a bit taller and stronger,
pull the scaffolding of myself together.

"What else do you think keeps me going
other than the idea that one day I will heal
from this collapsing thing I am trapped in?"

ALL OF LIFE IS A GARDEN

There are still roses
that will bloom in your lungs
if you can learn to breathe
through the thorns.

THIS IS HOW YOU WILL HURT

This is how you will hurt.

It will be a sunny day and you are still in your room, your curtains drawn to keep the light out, your body shaking under a blanket that just won't warm you up, but then again, you haven't felt warm since the day it happened. It is like he took every bit of warmth from your soul, and the only way you will ever feel warm again is if the entire sun grew inside of you.

Your mother is knocking on the door. You pretend you don't hear her. Your greatest deception since it happened is trying so hard to be normal, and today you do not have the energy for it.

Today, you are going to stare into the darkest corner of your room and wonder why the darkness doesn't do you a favor and swallow you whole.

This is how you will bleed.

You will only leave your house when the sky is filled with clouds and it is raining. You do not feel the need for warmth anymore. The only thing you feel is numb, your mind doing its bare minimum to hold itself together and your body doing its bare minimum to keep your bones from falling apart. You have become robotic in gestures, fluent in nothing but words and social cues.

"Hello."

"How are you?"

"I'm fine, thank you."

It is only when you walk by his house that your heart suddenly feels like it's trying to claw its way outside you, you feel hot and cold at once, your breath quickens and your stomach churns like you are being force-fed the universe and you can't say no—even though you are full. So you throw up, right there on the pavement, so close to his door.

Almost where it happened. But not quite.

This is how you will try.

Your parents will take you to a therapist because they are so tired of asking you what's wrong and you've run out of nothings to tell them. You've tried and they've tried, but the words just turn to ashes every time they try to leave your mouth. They start as fire in the pit of your stomach but come out in a puff of smoke.

So here you are sitting in front of a person you have never met before, a stranger you need to tell all your secrets to. And for an hour, you just sit there trying to find the words to speak, but when you can't even talk to your best friend, how do you speak to someone who doesn't even know how to pronounce your name properly?

You are not you anymore. And you don't know how to fix this. The worst part is…you don't even know how to try.

This is how it will end.

Everyone is tired of trying to get you to speak. So the doctors recommend a place for you to go. A place where they treat special cases like you.

It will be good. They promise. And when you come back, you will be better than ever—a new person almost. Recovery is a wonderful thing, you will see, when they open your mind up to understand what is wrong with you.

Recovery is a wonderful thing, they reassure you as you are led away to a car that doesn't belong to your parents, bile rising in your throat, but your body doing what it's told. You want to say no; you don't want to go.

But your mouth no longer knows how to speak for your heart, nor your soul. Because to you, recovery is not a wonderful thing.

Recovery is just an eight-letter word.

And so is insanity.

"I am fine" is just three words.

And so is: "He raped me."

THE
DESCENT

How do you kill a monster?

*You look for the frightened child
it once used to be.*

*Then you find a way
to set that child free.*

ON HURT

Deciding how hurt
someone is allowed to be
with your behavior
toward them
is the emotional
equivalent of:

1.
drowning someone
and deciding
how loud
they are allowed
to scream

2.
setting someone on fire
and deciding
how much of a mess
their ashes are allowed
to make

3.
stabbing someone
and deciding
how much
they are allowed
to bleed.

You do not get to
destroy someone
and decide how ruined
they are allowed to feel.

JUST GET OVER IT
(AND WHY YOU CAN'T)

Everyone tells you
to get over it,
and getting over it
is exactly what you're
trying to do.

But draining an ocean
is not easy.
It takes all the time
you can afford it
and then more than it is entitled to.

Learning how to release
the venom of suffering
from your soul
takes time, effort
and this is understood by so few.

A RECURRING NIGHTMARE/ EMOTIONAL ABUSE

There is
a monster.
There is a meal.

The monster
is you.
I am the meal.

And you take mouthfuls of me
huge, selfish as they are
leaving morsels of me behind

teeth my words and chew up my heart
devour through my spine with shark-like jaws
I am used, you explain, damaged,

You convince me I am unlovable. I am dirty.
Dirty for existing. I do not deserve better
And who will love me like this anyway?

I ask you why you like to hurt me
when all I have ever done is care for you. And you say cruelly,
"I love you most when you ache on the inside."

I have been trying for months to leave every day
but every time I do, you become human again
and force me to stay.

THE FALL

And my love, you will fall,
and you will fall hard,

every bone in your soul
will shatter a million times over.

But what you must remember
is every time you crash downwards,

you learn to stitch your spirit
back faster.

You learn to hold
these wind wings prouder and stretch them further.

You let the fall
make you stronger.

WHEN THEY CALL YOU NAMES BECAUSE YOU ARE DIFFERENT

So what if they misunderstand you,
they do not know how the suffering found you,
took your heart from your chest,
wore you in like a skin soon to be discarded,
turned you ragged, turned you into an almost husk,
made you into a half-self.
Yet, despite its efforts, you are still here,
pulling stronger selves out of a spine
within your spine,
sculpting a new you,
despite it trying to destroy you
every single day.
And that is what true courage looks like.
No matter what they say.

STARS AND YOU
EVOLVE IN SILENCE

At some point between their leaving
and your becoming,
you stop feeling.

And no, this is not a long-lasting,
painful sort of "I hope this ends"
because you've never been good at endings anyway.

This is worse. This is an "I feel nothing"
to the point that you know you should panic,
but even panic has deserted you.

You are dry.
Like a land that has had no water,
a barren lake, earth cracked by the sun.

And no one informs the ground how to look away
from the sun that is making it infertile, just like
no one informs you how to force feelings into a barren heart.

Call it a phase.
Call it a chapter.
But do not, whatever you do, call it shelter.

This is just what it feels like
to be the empty vessel the healing needs
to fill with the water that will make you feel like you belong.

THE SCARS YOU LEFT ON MY MIND WOULD LIKE A WORD WITH YOU

Look, there is no other way to say this,
but there is nothing kind in what you did to me.

You gutted me like a fish without touching me,
soft belly heart exposed, words like a knife.

At least I didn't put your hands on you,
I can hear you say when you read this.

And even on my darkest days, I admit,
sometimes my skin aches for your fingers

because the way you touched me was tender,
and gentle is something I have never known,

and you told me to be grateful
given my history with violent people.

As if prey should learn to
be grateful to be gutted by the hunter's knife.

As if a firefly caught and jarred
should be grateful for half a life.

THE APOLOGY YOU NEVER GOT

I apologize for every person
that loved you badly
and made you feel like
you take up more space than you deserve.

Nothing saddens me more
than watching you and knowing
they made you believe that love
is an awful thing that can only hurt.

DETACHMENT

When I was sixteen years old,
I stopped laughing. And no one could understand why. It was like the sun had pulled me out of bed one morning and told me the world can do without your laughter and your smiles.

People tried to fix me. They did this by deciding that getting a laugh from me was a competition, as if I was a thing so broken that every joke that fell upon my ears was just glue to set me back together.

Have you ever looked into a room full of people and thought, everything in there looks like a minefield, and I'd rather stay out here, in the silence because the quiet never made me feel like a broken thing, it only ever made me feel alone? This is how I understood the saying, the lesser of two evils.

I finally went to a therapist who told me "did you know when you fake laugh long enough, you automatically begin to really, really laugh?"

And when I tried it in front of the mirror, even though I did not believe her, and it worked, I was both happy and devastated.

Happy, because despite the still sad gleam in my eyes, in the end I learned how to fix myself.

Devastated, because that sad gleam was familiar. It told me how many people around me were fake laughing, too.

AN INEXPLICABLE PHOBIA

I read somewhere the other day
that phobias can be inherited,
and I guess this explains
the quiet fear that erupts in my chest
when I look at certain people
and I feel all my mother's panic
surge through my body,
as if my soul already knows
their intentions are less
than pure and true.

THE BRUTAL LESSON IN ESCAPE

Everyone who has ever run away
from their problems,
often thinks they have got far enough,
think they have finally found
a place they can call home,
a new beginning,
open a recently painted door
to their fresh start,
only to find every single problem
they ever had sitting there,
drinking cups of tea
without being invited
and waiting for them to walk through that door.

(The problem isn't that
they did not run far enough.
The problem is
they thought they could run at all.)

A SEASIDE STUDY

The other day by the seaside,
I saw a fish escape
the cruel beak of a seagull
because she refused
to stop struggling,
even in the very jaws of death,
and I wondered,
if I will one day
learn to be as brave
as that fish.

THE THING THAT BURNS ALL IT LOVES

To all the people who grew
tired of waiting for me
to stop being a thing that burned them
when they got too close
to learn how to stop pushing their love away,
who deserved better than the half-love than I could give them,
who told me that being with me was emotional torture,
who said "your heart is in the right place,

but for the sake of all that is holy, fix your mind,"
who only had the best in their hearts for me
and who I didn't treat right,
I want you to know I did it.
I finally walked to the doctor's office

instead of sitting in a car outside
and just counting the streetlights.

He told me that
"Depression is a silent killer;
it convinces you that you are fine
whilst you are at the edge of a building
and tells you to take your life."

He asked me,
"How long have you been
a thing that burns everything?"

And I said,
out loud for the first time,
finally admitting to myself,
"All of my life."

A LOST LANGUAGE

There is a language on my tongue
that I didn't even know lived there.
I call it by your love, I call it you.

It is all the softness
I learned about you
and all the seconds you meant to me.

Tell me how to untangle
and unlanguage you
from my lips

when you
are caught on my tongue
in every single word I speak.

FOUR LIES I UNLEARNED:

I.

Nothing is bone-dry
because if you strip us down
to our living skeletons
we are still a third water.

II.

Money can in fact
buy happiness when you spend
everything you have buying someone you love
the thing they have needed for years.

III.

It actually takes more muscles
to smile than frown.
Ask anyone who has been
masking their deepest pain with a smile.

IV.

It is absolutely possible
to love someone deeply, purely, wholly
whilst still learning, struggling, understanding
how to love yourself.

A BEE'S STING

Be as fierce as a bee.
Protect the thing
you love most
even if your death comes to be.

And it is only
by learning fearlessness that
you will finally reap
who you are, heart golden as honey.

NOTE TO SELF 456

The scars aren't beautiful.
The courage of the person
who wears them so gracefully is.

THE TEN BREAKUP TEXTS I SHOULD HAVE SENT YOU BUT DIDN'T

I.

How do I say this poetically: You fucking destroyed me.

2.

The number of calls from you on my phone is zero. The number of calls from me to you is one. When you hear the voicemail, I hope you don't hear the desperation in the way I wish you all the luck in the world and tell you how pleased I am for you. I hope you don't hear the way my lungs breathe "iloveyouineedyoupleasedontgo" very time I draw in a breath.

3.

I am so determined to be the girl who lets you go so that you can come back, I forget to accommodate for the fact that sometimes wild things do not return, not even for their young, and you and I have no such bond or hold on each other.

4.

I only learned that I was a cage when I realized I was in love with someone who was in love with someone else and would rather lie than tell me.

5.

I have also learned that three days of alcohol-induced slumber is still not enough to get rid of every sugar-spun dream I have of you. It is still a shock when I reach for you in the mornings and you are not there.

6.

There are a thousand poems in the way you left a girl with so much hope that she no longer knows how to breathe promise without it ringing with your name.

7.

I am still tasting forevers in the way your eyes meet mine, even though your lips are using words like "space" and "travel" and "promise." And I am nodding because I understand, when I was a little girl, I set free a cage of captured birds in my aunt's home, because there is something in the way birds fly after captivity that makes them seem almost holy.

8.

It was the way your lip curled on the word "promise" that makes me uncomfortable. There are only three other people in my life that have ever used that word, and they are all strangers now.

9.

I am learning to accept that caged birds never return to say thank you when they are set free, and not everything that flies after captivity deserves to be called holy.

10.

I hope the forever you found in her doesn't turn to ash like it did with me. I hope wherever you are in this world that you are truly happy.

THE
ACCEPTANCE

I suppose
I love my scars
because they have
stayed with me
longer
than most people
have.

KINTSUGI

On the days when you feel ashamed
of your scars,

your mind only registering
how ugly they are rather than
the beauty they prove of you
having survived,

remember that there is an entire art
form dedicated to filling
the cracks of broken things
with lacquered gold.

An entire art form that proves
that even the broken and damaged history
of an object is beautiful and should be treasured.
Remember how much more you are than an object.

Remember that your survival,
your journey,
your scars
deserve to be treasured, too.

A LESSON IN GRATITUDE

I learned this the hard way
on truly awful days,
when all your brain
can focus on is the dreadful things
that have happened to you,

it is a gift to be able
to focus and concentrate
on the wonderful
and much bigger things
that were given to you.

Slowly, they make the bad days
turn sheepish
and slowly slink away,
and you feel better
for winning back the day.

ABOUT SELF LOVE

Self-love
is accountability.

Self-love
is self-critique.

Self-love
is reflection.

Self-love
is practicing honesty.

Self-love
is tough love.

If it was supposed to be easy,
they would call it self-enablement,
not self-love.

THE TRUTH ABOUT YOUR HEART

Your heart will fix itself.
It's your mind you need to worry about.
Your mind where you locked the memories,
your mind where you have kept pieces
of the ones that hurt you
that still cut through you
like shards of glass.

Your mind will keep you up at night,
make you cry,
destroy you over and over again.

You need to convince your mind that it has to let go...
because your heart
already knows how to heal.

THE SEA AND I

I don't think the sea
ever really meant to become so big.
She just went out there
and took up as much space as she could.

Weathered entire cliffs,
made beaches out of lands
so they could make way for her
in her fullness.

There was no apology in it for anyone,
she took the room that she needed.
And when the ships became
too many trying to explore her vastness,

she swallowed them
and held them as wreckages inside herself.
From the sea I have learned
to embrace all of my own glory.

Even when I think it is ugly,
take up the space I need in this world,
become everything that I am afraid to be,
and when the wreckage comes,

and it will,
welcome it whole, keep it in my belly,
forever mine, but never a tragedy.

FORGIVENESS SPEAKS

It says:

Forgiveness is what you must drink first
take the nectar in cupped hands
and quench your own thirst.

It says:

This is how you allow your heart and mind to heal
from trusting the heart and arms
you fell into that did you so much harm.

It says:

Even a lion will think all it is worth
is a circus cage and a whip for a home
if that is all it has ever known.

IN WHICH I ADMIT
I HAVE LOVED BADLY

Perhaps the actual problem is the inexcusable way
I have taught myself how to love people.

If my heart was a flower, it would be
an anomaly born without sepal or petals.

Who pieces of my soul-gold invested
inside the bank of someone else's heart.

I mean, Aphrodite never shows up at school,
book in hand, teaching love as the only real art.

There are no classes in coping with the loss
of whole people, no warnings left on memory's tombs.

They say love is what makes the world go round,
but no one ever leaves a note for us in the womb.

No instruction manual when we are born,
nor a how-to guide on the correct way to fall.

Nor one on how to barter pieces of yourself
without losing an eternity inside someone else's soul.

I'm afraid this is why I have always been so lost.
I have been loved, and I have loved

but I never learned how to gracefully bear the cost.

PEOPLE SURVIVE
IN DIFFERENT WAYS

Some people survive to talk about it.
Some people survive it and go silent.
Some people survive it and create.
Everyone deals with unimaginable pain
in their own way,
and everyone is entitled to that,
without judgment.

So next time you look at someone's life covetously,
remember…you may not want to endure
what they are enduring right now,
at this moment,
whilst they sit so quietly before you,
looking like a calm ocean on a sunny day.

Remember how vast the ocean's boundaries are.
Whilst somewhere the water is calm,
in another place in the very same ocean,
there is a colossal storm.

THE TRUTH ABOUT LETTING GO

What you must know about letting go is this:
It hurts. More than anything, it hurts.

Don't believe the lies they tell you
when they say letting go will fix every wound.

It is not like the wounds signed a contract
with the pain and said, "This date, this moment it ends.

After this, everything will automatically heal
and grief will no longer wear this skin,"

because darling, if it was that easy,
why would so many of us be broken?

So many of us are unable to let go of the things
that then become the demons that haunt our sins.

We are all both water and dam,
holding onto our pain unspoken,

afraid that if we fully let go will we be flooded with dis-
like for the people we see when we have broken open.

This is why letting go will be
the most courageous thing you will do.

Because once you let go,
you have to get to know a new you, a different you.

A QUESTION THAT HAUNTS

How many people do you think
we have loved alive
and then destroyed
because they didn't turn out to be
who we expected them to be?

ANSWER:
Did you really think
you were completely innocent
of breaking people's hearts?

WHY LOVING AGAIN
IS SO PAINFUL

Humans learn nothing from history
we teach it in our high schools
and debate about it in university,
but never ever apply it to our lives.

You see, we fall in love,
and when that love leaves,
we panic and give our hearts a shove,
when it's only just learning to survive.

We keep walking into love again
And again without cauterizing
the wounds and the pain
of our hearts' last breaking.

This is why loving again
feels like salt on open wounds.
This is why trusting again
feels like bodies made
of old deceit and betrayal
being constantly exhumed.

TO THE BARTENDER IN ST. LOUIS WHO GAVE ME THE BEST ADVICE I NEVER LISTENED TO

Thank you for the whiskey
that night when I needed
to forget the destruction quickly.

I'm sorry I never did learn
how to give up people
before they hurt me beyond repair.

I still listen when people tell me
that they will change.
I've forgiven more mistakes than I should.

I kept my heart soft,
if a little more bruised than ever before
a little more worn to the touch.

I know that love isn't meant
to be permanently damaging.
I've just tried to use my love too often

to aid other people's healing.
I'm learning to get better.
I try harder every day.

But maybe part of being me
was always to give people the kind
of love I wish someone would give to me.

WATER

When they ask you
why you love the rain,
the ocean, the river,
tell them it is because
unlike the people
who should have loved you better,
the water was never afraid to touch you;
even when you were
at your most damaged
and broken.

WHAT THE TOXIC PEOPLE
DO NOT KNOW

Here you are
in a pool of toxicity
surrounded by people
intent to throw you in the dirt,
hoping that you will not
find your way out
they do not know
in your fist
you still hold
the seeds of hope
and no matter how thick
the mud they toss you in,
you are the lotus,
brighter petaled
and stem stronger
back again
you will grow.

A FOREST STORY

There is an entire forest
full of the most incredible flowers,
plants, and trees inside you,
and you are ignoring all of it
to nurture a single tree
that they planted
inside your heart
and abandoned.

The people who left you this way
don't deserve to become
your favorite stories to tell.
You are a massive forest
full of beautiful and vibrant
stories and every single one of them
deserves you more
than those that abandoned
you to hell.

A FOREST STORY II

On the days
you name yourself empty,
think your existence
is a sum total
of small catastrophes,
think,
why did I happen
to this world
and what difference
could just one person
possibly make,
just remember
that there is a man
in the North of India
who turned a stretch
of 1,360 acres of land
into a forest single-handedly.
Accept that you
are a thing of great potential
and your purpose
is to leave
something greater
than yourself
on this earth,
on this soft mother.

THE DAY YOU LEFT

The day you left, I began to read space theories. I read about why the earth goes around the sun, about the solar system slowly collapsing into itself, about black holes and supernovas. But the truth is, the more I read about the universe, the more they began to blend together into a pastiche of you, of me, of us. This isn't about spirituality, understand. This isn't about how "it wasn't in the stars" and "I wish I had loved you like the earth loves the sun". I have already written those poems for you and the image of you walking away from a home that was once ours helped me understand that there is no romance in the way a star collapses. It is ugly to watch a thing of beauty turn on itself.

The day you left, I learned that some black holes roam at nine hundred miles an hour searching for things to absorb into their abyss—entire planets like ours, entire solar systems have disappeared into their shark-like mouths. And I found you shaped like a black hole the first night I had to sleep without you and tried to reach for you. It sucked me in, into its graveyard of stars leaving me there for no one to find. It took me three days to find my way back, to leave our bed, to call my mother back and try to explain where I have been. I lost her, as I would lose anyone between empty explanations of black holes and supernovas.

The day you left, I forgot how to write. I forgot the way it feels to have my fingers wrap around a pen and pour emotions in black ink into a white abyss of nothingness— filling it with words so that it doesn't seem so empty…so terrifyingly alone. Do you remember my fear of wide-open blank spaces, both dark and light? You told me that blank white nothingness is what it feels like to be at the center of a star just as it is falling apart. I'm so sorry I didn't believe you. I am there now, and I know you weren't lying.

The day you left, I read that the earth once upon a time may have had a second moon. That the moon we see to-day was created by the collision between the two. It helps me realize that sometimes, there is beauty in destruction. It helps me realize that sometimes the most beautiful things are built from accidents or collisions. And that is where I will leave our love. On an oasis between super-nova and a black hole, a safe place lost between the two.

THE TRUTH ABOUT MONSTERS

The truth is this:
Every monster
you have met
or will ever meet
was once a human being
with a soul
that was as soft
and light
as silk.

Someone stole
that silk from their soul
and turned them
into this.

So when you see
a monster next
always remember
do not fear
the thing before you;
fear the thing
that created it
instead.

THE DIFFERENCE BETWEEN ALONE AND LONELY

I.

You and your love are both soft and haunted and some people will come into your life and take that softness for granted. This is just how the world is, my darling, diamonds exist but so do wolves and sometimes it is the diamonds that we need to watch out for because they are made of cold and wolves still have heartbeats and are just misunderstood. Navigating the world is a hard thing, especially for girls who are made of story-flavored madness and seeking happy endings here that are harder than finding a pearl in the deepest part of the ocean.

2.

I have known of too many girls who have both become and died in the embrace of men that should have loved them better but chose to let them go. Both gods and men tend to treat dreamers and romantics with an equal part of disdain and neglect. I have ached for them, but watching sadness does things to a person's mind and heart.

3.

My cousin was a small girl with dreams the size of a country and determination made of a bullet that penetrated every job she ever did. I never once saw her fail and then she fell in love. Even bullets can dissolve when put in enough heat. Watching her melt from a gun to a wound was enough to teach me that alone had a lovely sound to it.

4.

Alone and lonely are two different things. Alone means nights with my books. Alone means quiet stargazing and drinking tea on my roof. Alone means hours of self-aware retrospection in a coffee shop whilst scribbling poetry. But most importantly alone means not wilting into the arms of a man who may not appreciate the stars and poetry. Lonely is carnal. Lonely is craven. Lonely is sad.

5.

I thought I was safe in my alone. But love is a wicked predator; it found my hiding place even in a forest. To do so, it set my beautiful forest of alone on fire.

6.

For a while, we were happy. For a while, love almost had me believing that I was wrong. Until the day you left like a hurricane leaves the ocean. For good.

7.

I crumbled. Picked myself up. And crumbled again. Eventually I lost track of how many times I had to get up. Eventually you began to fade into the graveyard of the still living people that have abandoned me in my head.

8.

I am better now. The forest of my alone finally has grown back from the ashes. Bigger and better than before, my alone is beautiful. It is slowly filling the graves you left inside me with self-love and healing. This version of alone is softer with my heart than your love has ever left it feeling.

THE
DEFIANCE

Never forget,
you are more powerful
than you are damaged
and you will rise
from any abyss
they drown you in.

A WAR NAMED YOU

This will be visceral.
There will be no apology.
When you are a hunted thing
you long learn that
apologies
were not built for you.
So you learn to become
the hunter.
Teach your bones
the magic. The music.
You will be no lamb
to the slaughter.

So what if you are only human?
You can turn brutal people
into cautionary tales
by raising your voice.

You just need to learn the art
of thunder.
The craft of soft war.

WHAT TO SAY WHEN THEY THINK YOU HAVE COME TO THEM FOR VALIDATION

My witchcraft
does not answer to you.

I did not come here
for your validation,
for your words
to bring out the best in me,
when I am already
the best I can be.

I came here
to tell you my magic is mine
and mine alone.
You can love me
or hate me,

but this is how I was made,
thunder skinned
and lightning boned.

I BET THEY DIDN'T EXPECT IT

A thing this free is never
expected anywhere.

I think this is why
we are always surprised
when we see a stag in the wild
even though this is where a stag
is supposed to be.

I always aspired to be a stag's leap
and not a doe's eyes
when she is caught in the headlights,
and that is what
they wanted me to be.

Listen.

The acid in my stomach
did not learn how
to dissolve razor blades
for me to fall prey to you.

My heart is not a warrior's fist
so that it falls apart
at a predator's touch.
I was made of fight and fearsome
before I was made for love and lust.

I know this is a surprise to you,
but my mother raised her fawn as a wolf cub
to take on everything.
This is who I am,
a song of softness and savagery,

teeth and claws at the ready,
and if I were you
I would be careful because
I was born with a war
caught inside my fists.

Do not approach me
if you think you
cannot handle all of this.

RAISE YOUR DAUGHTERS

Raise your daughters
to shout,
to scream,
to hold their heads
up high for being themselves
before society
tries to teach them
how to silence themselves,
how to wear shame
like it is a second skin.

Raise them
to take on
entire armies
with fearless ease,
command battalions
of confidence,
build them armor
made from a mother's love,
give them swords
made of their father's belief.

Let them taste rebellion
from the moment
they are born
and watch them
become flames
to start a revolution.

FOR THE EARTH

Listen to the world
falling apart
right under our feet.
Listen to the earth
thundering
and asking
for us to help
it become
what it is
supposed to be.

Listen to our mother
asking us to be
kinder to it,
to hold it close
as it weeps.
They've been
invalidating her, too,
the way they invalidate
all trauma survivors
telling her that
her fears are not real.

Gaslighting her
by telling her
that her oceans
will self-heal
from oil spills,
that the bruise
on her atmosphere
is all in her head.

If there were ever
a time to become
a hurricane,
an earthquake,
a volcano,
this is it.
Now is no longer
the time to sleep.

THE REBELLIOUS OPTIMIST

I have this completely
unwavering belief
and some people
call me crazy
when they hear it,
which is, one day we will all
come to a point as a species
where we recognize hatred
for exactly what it is,
a lying and corrupt sorcerer,
standing in our way,
stopping us all
from passing the threshold
to becoming better for each other,
from doing better,
unchampioning
every truly good human
from doing good work,
take it by the lapels
and throw it off this planet
whilst saying in unison,
"Love wins, love truly wins,
now and forever more."

PERMISSION

The universe does not take permission
from the starts or the planets
before it creates something new.
It evolves entire solar systems
and galaxies full of life.

And you are its masterpiece.
Freshly constructed from
Four billion years of undefeated
ancestry traced all the way back
to single-celled organisms.

You do not need to take permission
and explain away your existence
when the universe made
whole planets and galaxies
and collected their blood to form you.

THE RECLAIMATION

(After Amanda Lovelace's
The Witch Doesn't Burn In This One)

"Bitch."
The seemingly violent word eclipses
My nonviolent walk home
because I dared to ignore you.

I used to wither, you know.
Used to be crushed under the weight
when they spoke words like that
specifically to dehumanize me.

No more. I refuse to be damaged
by the words of shallow-spirited men
birthed from the very wombs
they do not respect.

You called me a bitch,
so now I wear it as a coronet
reclaim every insult you throw
and you ain't seen nothing yet.

You've just made me angry
prompted the animal hiding
inside my rib cage, so take
these words as fair warning:

Never again trivialize
the power of my sisters and I
because you only do it out of fear
of women stronger than you.

And you know what bitches do
when they smell fear, don't you?

We howl.
And then we hunt.

AN ODE TO FEARLESS WOMEN

I think your bones
were made in an elsewhere place.

How else does one explain
this inconceivable strength that makes you?

The way you looked into danger's mouth
and saw no cemetery or death.

Instead, you carved your name into
its teeth with a switchblade,

defeated it so effortlessly and
threw your head back and laughed.

Paradox girl, mighty woman,
you are the thing that terrifies them.

Both monster and maiden, both cure and poison,
all of these things, and at the same time woman.

Defined by no man, you are your own story,
blazing through the world, turning history into herstory.

And when they dare to tell you about
all the things you cannot be,
you smile and tell them,
"I am both war and woman and you cannot stop me."

THE QUEST FOR AUTHENTICITY

I have always liked my people a bit damaged.
A bit rough around the edges. A bit difficult to stereotype.
A bit stranger than the normal crowd.

I like people whose eyes tell stories and whose smiles have fought through wars. If you're perfect, chances are we aren't going to get on. If you're one of the cool kids, chances are, you won't like me. You see, what I want is authentic. What I want to see is your purity; I want to see the way you wear your scars, I want to see how brave you are with your vulnerability, how emotionally naked you let the world see you. Your damage may not be beautiful, but it has made you exquisite. It makes you original, different—and one of my kind of people because people like you are the most incredible things about this world.

RELY ON YOUR
OWN LOVE INSTEAD

If they choose not to hold you,
remind yourself you
do not need his arms.
Not when you have two
of your own.
Hold yourself.
Remind yourself
that the love you
have to give is more nurturing
than he can ever give you,
and you deserve that love,
a far more wholesome love than theirs.

HOW TO BE AN ABUSE SURVIVOR IN A WORLD THAT HATES SURVIVORS

1.

Know that they will tell you, no matter the bruises, no matter the wounds, no matter how many people back you up, that somehow, somewhere along the way this was your fault. You could have gotten away, and you chose not to. Know also that they are lying, because you lived it and they didn't.

2.

When the abuse comes back to haunt you like it is a ghost inside a haunted house that has been torn down and is trying to resurrect itself, do not chase it away. Instead, tell it that you remember. Tell it that each splintered bone that holds your mind together is still aching and cry on this together.

3.

When you go through the moments where you are questioning yourself whether or not it was abuse, remember the way it made you feel. Push away the nostalgia that is trying to minimize it, trying to trick you like a bad magician at a children's party that the rabbit did come from the hat, that love and abuse come out of the same hat.

4.

At some point your parents will ask why. Why you didn't trust them. Why you didn't come to them. How they let you down. Hold your mother first, because she really needs to know she is not a burning building. Then hold your father and remind him that once a baby bird has grown and flown away, their pain, and their burdens are their own and no one can protect them from this. Not even the forest. Not even their parents' love.

5.

Remind yourself over and over again how it was not your fault for not leaving sooner. That your mind had you convinced that the abuse was the blip between good times. How even the earth makes mistakes in timing and there are some plants that do not flower, they only sprout to saplings and die. This is what life is. A deconstruction of errors into lessons. This makes you no less valid.

6.

When you hear people whisper against you, remember that the reason they are whispering is because even their tongues and voices are aware that what they are doing is wrong, and they whisper their lies because their voices know guilt.

7.

If it feels like they were never punished for what they did to you; remind yourself that punishment is not always visible to the eye. That orchids may look pretty but they are still nothing but parasites. That they may look well, but you, you are better. At least the inside of you is still a place where things can grow without relying on harming anyone else. At the very least, you are still a heart beating honestly, peacefully without relying on the pain of someone else.

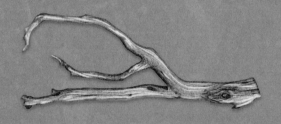

THE
SURVIVAL

*How else will your soul
make space for the enormous
task of healing if you never ever
allow yourself to crumble,
to let that tough facade crack?*

*You are holding those broken pieces
so tightly to your chest,
you can't see how
they are piercing
your heart*

THE CELEBRATION

Celebrate yourself.
Just celebrate your heart
and your soul
and all those little things
about you no one knows.

This world is already
made of too many humans
that do not know
how to love themselves
because they do not know
how to look at themselves
in a mirror and say,

"I am a brutal thing
made of flowers,
and that is how
I will survive
everything
whilst still being soft."

Learn how to do that,
because you will have
that elusive myth
people constantly
talk about,
self-love.

Most days,
you will feel like
you are decorating
a decaying thing
with flowers.

Many days,
you will know
the stink of pain
under the scent
of happiness.

Some days, though,
you will emerge
as glory and gold
and surprise
even yourself.

Those are the days
you will be grateful
you held on.

Those are the days
that your survival
feels like both
a love song
and a war song.

YOU CAN LIVE
THROUGH ANYTHING

If you think you
do not think
you will get out
of this one alive,

just remember,
you could remove
a large part of your internal organs
and still survive.

No person,
nothing is too big
for you
to live through,

you already know
how to live through
everything truly painful
and still thrive.

LEARNING THROUGH SEEING

If you are coming to these arms
seeking the glue
that will put back your broken pieces,
then forgive me,
for these arms will let you down.

But this heart knows
the secret you seek,
and I will show you in full,
how I took my own brokenness
from inside my body,

how I learned to look at it
and not think of it as ugly,
how I listened to it rage and blame,
how when it finally
had no more words to say,

I told it that I loved it,
that I was no longer afraid of it,
that it did not have to live in the shadows,
that it had a place instead inside me.
A home and a name.

WHO YOU WERE
VS. WHAT YOU ARE

Somewhere in your childhood,
someone you once loved
betrayed your whole little heart
and told you that you were not enough.

And because thoughts become things,
it became ivy inside your mind and body
until this was all you believed about yourself
and your self-worth became mutiny.

Remember that the stars and planets did not die
for you to waste your time wondering
if you are pretty enough
or worthy enough to exist.

You are still trying, in this body,
to be all the things that make a person.
But the truth is you are bursting at the seams
because you are a plethora of universes becoming a human.

WILD FORCES

There are wild forces at work here,
if you do not believe me
ask the sun and its melody,
you'll find it hidden in its rays.

It will tell you the same thing
the rain always sings
when the drops hit the surface
sounding like applause and praise.

These are secrets to your existence
hidden all over nature
an elemental treasure hunt
to remind you the universe is there.

This is its way of holding you close,
teaching you to not give up your existence
reminding you that the thing that created
you gave you this chance because it cares.

ANCESTRAL WISDOM

We are all the sons and daughters
of astronomers,
ancestors who saw God
talking to them through
every star in the soft velvet sky.

They believed that God
was leaving them messages
telling them to be strong
on nights when the entire world's
voice felt like an endless cry.

The cosmos is an elastic expanse
made from infinite stories.
Our ancestors, their descendants
all atoms in a fairytale embroidery
that shimmers across our memory scars.

Perhaps this is why we all love the stars;
we see in that patchwork canvas of time
a sense of who we used to be
who we are going to become
and who we truly are.

A LESSON FROM SATURN

Saturn would float if you put it in water.
An entire planet built of
such self-confidence
that even if someone tries to drown it
it refuses to give up.

Perhaps then, the idea is not just to survive.
It is to make yourself of such strength
that if they ever try to destroy you
you use their own instruments of betrayal
against them and thrive.

CHALK AND COAL

The earth has always
believed in reincarnation.
The fossilized bones
of sea creatures make up the chalk
we use on our blackboards.
The ancient forests that once
were giants on its surface
are now the coal we use for warmth.

So why do we believe our energy
has been wasted on those
who chose not to love us in return?
Nothing you truly feel for another
is ever wasted; instead it is reincarnated,
turned into fuel that propels us to being
the thing we need today rather
than the thing we were yesterday.

This is why we call it evolution.
This is why we call it growth.

YOU ARE GOOD DESIGN

Nothing about you is wrong,
no matter how much the
world tries to convince you
these details of you are unwanted.

The softness in your being
is because a little macrocosm
resides there and macrocosms
need forgiving places to exist.

The faith in your spirit
is because the stars need you
to believe in them; they gave up
their glow to bring yours to life.

That riptide of energy about you
that people call too much to handle
is the same glorious energy that has
existed since the Big Bang happened.

You are a group of particles constructed
into a being that lives for a second
yet leaves a lasting effect on
the atoms around you.

You were brought to life by something
so powerful that with the odds stacked
against you of one in gazillions
that you were still a great idea.

You are good design in function
in motion, in ability
and everything you believe ordinary
about you is simply extraordinary.

AN UPDATE FROM
THE ONE YOU LEFT

Since you made the shift from "my love"
To "a thing that once happened to me,"
a lot has changed.

I am still trying to find the remedy
to loneliness, of course, but my smile
is at last convincing to strangers.

I no longer need everything to mean
more than what it is; sometimes missing
someone is just that.

And even though sometimes the bed
feels like a desert of emptiness without you,
I do not want you back.

Even my mother has noticed
I look less like a struggle caught inside
my skin every day.

I have learned to save blissful moments
inside capsules that I will eat later
when the sadness comes to stay.

And I understand now that the absence of tragedy
makes room for the growth of happiness
and this is what it truly means to be human.

What I am trying to say is:
I promised you in front of our God
that I would live through our ruins.

So here I am.
As promised.
Healing. Breathing. Living.

THE WAY DAMAGED PEOPLE LOVE

Damaged people love you like you are a crime scene
before a crime has even been committed.
They keep their running shoes by their souls every night,
one eye open in case things change whilst they sleep.
Their backs are always tense as though waiting
to fight a sudden storm that might engulf them.

Because damaged people have already seen hell.

And damaged people understand that every evil demon
that exists down there was once a kind angel before it fell.

SICKLE MOONS OF HOPE

I have always been
the kind of person
that searches for sickle moons
of hope inside
even the darkest
of human monsters
because no one ever taught me
that some people
are simply rogue planets
—moonless and soulless.

And this has forever
been my greatest undoing.

LESSONS I LEARNED
ABOUT GROWING UP

Grow up. Be successful,
even if no one truly knows what that means.
Teach your spine that it still
has the capacity to grow feathers and fly
even when the world slowly
starts revealing itself as anything but a sky.

Fall in love for the first time.
Name them the horizon.
Name them the stars above.
Let them break your heart unutterably.
Do not listen when everyone else
names this indescribable force
that awoke your soul "puppy love."

Surrender your body to yourself.
Do not give society any control
when they try to turn you
into a map of their whims and fancies.
Reclamation of yourself will be
your first small act of revolt.

Survive the tragedies.
Learn that the sum of a person lies both
in the way they treat those

who have nothing to give them in strife
and in the way they lift themselves
off the ground after a bar fight with life.

Learn that the trouble
is growing up complicates everything.
That people say "only human"
as though being human is a small thing to be.
Until you learn the truth
about the celestial violence, an impossibility.

Get better at losing people.
Get better at losing parts of yourself.
Get used to knowing
that everyone is temporary,
learning that growing up
is choosing between ways
that will break you in two selves.

Just because other people have hurt you,
you do not have to be cruel.
But if you are, apologize.
Make amends. Become a better you.
Don't wear your heart on your sleeve;
wear your softness as a crown.

Listen to who you were when you were young.
Become the skyscraper

you thought you were going to be.
Become every bedtime story
that ended with a smile, not a frown.

You see, today I found a note
from my seven-year-old self.
All it read was, "When I grow up,
I just want to be a good human."
And all I could think was,
"I really hope I haven't let her down."

YOU ARE A MIRACLE

On your worst days, when the world has been most cruel to you, when things have gone so wrong you can barely breathe without a thousand knives feeling like they are stabbing into you and you feel like you don't matter, that none of this matters, I hope you look at the night sky. I hope you realize that in that moment of looking at the incredible tapestry before you that you are not alone. And most importantly, I hope you understand how no matter what the world has done to you that day, you are a deeply essential being.

You see that same thing that has made the beautiful night sky, with all its diamond stars, with its luminous moon, with the millions of solar systems and galaxies that exist side by side, also thought that you were a brilliant idea. And this isn't just a pretty thing to say; there is science to back that up. The probability of you existing at all comes down to 1 in 10 to the power of 2,685,000.

The very idea that you exist considering those extremely low odds is a miracle on its own. You see, the exact DNA that comes from your parents to create you could have only happened when your parents met, which is 1 chance in 20,000. That alone should be enough, but when you add up the fact that it has taken 5-10 million years of human evolution for you to exist at this time, in this moment, you begin to recognize just how much of an impossibility you are.

And look, look at what your body is made of. The universe loved you so much, it valued your fight to exist so much, that it gave you the blood of stars, so you are made of 93 percent of the very stars in that night sky. It gave you acids within your stomach that eat away anything you cannot digest including the hateful emotions that are thrown your way. It gave you a heart that is so powerful it can beat outside of your body. It gave you a spine stronger than granite. It gave you iron in your veins to remind you of the warrior you are.

You weren't supposed to exist. You fought all of those odds just to be here. And that is no accident. You are here for a reason. You breathe this air for a reason. You have purpose; your existence means something. Someone smiled because of you today. Someone remembered something you did that was kind. Someone went to sleep thinking of you today. And moreso, there ARE people who love you and people you haven't met yet who will love you so much, they would do anything for you.

You are a miracle. The idea of your existence is a miracle. The fact that you are breathing at all is a miracle. Remember this when the world makes you feel like you don't matter.

The universe who is creator to us all thought you were a brilliant plan. So it gave you a chance to breathe and exist even when the probability was so very low, all because you fought to be here and never gave up. From the moment it thought of you, you had already won a cosmic war.

Don't stop fighting now. No matter what your mental illness says, no matter what the world tells you, no matter the odds. You get up, you look at that night sky, you remember every star that collapsed its own lungs to bring you to life, you remember their sacrifice, and you get up and fight again.

THE
WORSHIP

"Where did all the Gods go?"

"The humans," she answered quietly,
"They turned them all into
stories and bone."

HOW TO BECOME A MYTH

I.

Fly into the sun,
defy anyone who tells you
that you cannot love Him.

The ocean will break your fall,
even if it is by drowning you.

(You knew he would burn you, Icarus;
you simply thought he was worth the risk.)

2.

Get stolen by a God,
run away with him,
away from the meadows, wood nymph.

Become Queen of the underworld.
Turn the land of the dead into home.

(You knew, didn't you, Cora?
How you would rather be Persephone?)

3.

Turn yourself into an echo
of the person you used to be,
then fall in love with him.

And when he doesn't notice you
and instead falls in love with himself, pine away.

(Narcissus could never love you, dear Echo.
Not the way he loved himself.)

4.

Become an indestructible monster.
Become the thing that warriors speak of
in hushed breaths in terror.

When you finally do die at someone's hands,
make sure it is glorious.

(Theseus was the only end
worthy of you, Minotaur.)

5.

When the Sea God assaults you,
turn people into stone.
Turn Gods into stone.

Turn anything that threatens you
ever again into stone.

(Medusa, Athena turned you ugly to protect you.
She took your beauty to give you power.)

6.

Adore her so much that the world
grieves with
your broken heart's song.

Almost save her
from the underworld. Almost.

(Orpheus, all you had to do
was not turn to look at her.)

7.

Marry a God King.
Watch him betray you over and over again.
Become bitter and cruel.

Recognize he will never respect you.
Promise to make him suffer till he does.

(Hera, I know why you couldn't leave him;
it was all for love, it was all for love.)

8.

Become an undefeated warrior
in a war where you lose
everything you love.

Even the one you love most of all.
Don't realise it. Keep fighting.

(Achilles, Patroclus's love would
have made you immortal, anyway.)

9.

Be unhappy in your marriage.
Find a dangerous prince
who promises you a real love.

Run away with him.
Do not think of the consequences.

(Helen, you didn't just launch a thousand ships;
you set kingdoms ablaze.)

10.

Destroy everyone
you love
in a murderous rage.

Go on a journey
hoping it will kill you.

(Hercules tell the truth, you hoped those tasks
would be your destruction, didn't you?)

Addendum:
Don't become a myth.
Stay human.
Stay mortal.

It is less wounds.
I promise. It is less wounds.

A CONVERSATION
WITH THE SUN GOD

I have been speaking with the Sun God lately,
about you and about me and about how
your love for me is like Icarus's for him.

I mention grieving.
I mention sadness.
I mention loss.

And he sighs and says,
"But people like us have always
burned the ones we love."

I wonder if the place in your heart
I used to have has slowly become a wound
instead where I burned through to get out.

Apollo reminds me how Icarus
was the only mortal to ever try to touch him.
He was the only mortal who ever dared to love him.

I look away
because I understand,
even if I am no God.

Sometimes we hurt the people we love most,
not because we want to,
but because no one has ever dared to come this close.

No one ever truly
wants someone else
to see their frayed soul.

So Apollo still carries Icarus's heart.
And I still carry every memory of what we were
and how we fell apart.

CORA DOESN'T LIVE HERE ANYMORE

Keep your pity.

Keep your stories of a girl stolen
from her mother's woods,
as if she was nothing but a child
who could not defend herself,
I knew exactly what I was doing,
when he came to get me.

Keep your tales about
a hideous villain named Hades,
when my King has the eyes of a storm,
a wicked smile fashioned
from both hurricane and a nebula bursting
and I gave my heart to him willingly.

Do not tell me about
how I had no violence in these bones,
no ambition in my eyes,
just a soft, pretty thing a God stole
and made his queen,
a girl forever sad and lonely.

Perhaps you have not heard of my legacy,
I make those who hurt him beg for mercy,
I hunt monstrous men and torture them to my fancy,
I bring the dead back to life if I deem them worthy,

I have the whole underworld at my feet,
and you have the gall to think I am unhappy?

You must be mistaken by my mother's tales
of her darling daughter Cora, my dear.
The only one who lives here now
is the one I was always destined to be,
Queen of the underworld,
the Goddess Persephone.

ECHO GETS OVER NARCISSUS
IN THIS VERSION

Narcissus Rejects Echo For The Last Time: *Echo Responds:*

Let me be clear, I will never love you,   You

I was made for worship and you were   were

made for silly little stories where the   the

women simply pined away with ache   ache

for part-man/part-elf like me, you lucky in   in

simply meeting and knowing me, for my   my

beauty is a gift from the gods and my bones   bones,

were crafted by Aphrodite herself until   until

Zeus took me from her reluctant arms so I   I

was blessed with his might, and I learned   learned

then that the gods themselves knew how   how

essential I was going to be to mortals, so to   to

you, nymph, I say your heart should unlove   unlove

me for it is too small for me; take your   your

wretched presence away before I become cruel.   cruel.

HOW ASTERION
BECAME THE MINOTAUR

(It was not supposed to end this way.)

No one remembers it anymore,
but you were born gentle under the sickle moon,
a sweetness about you that made your mother's heart sway.

They never told you that you were supposed
to grow up to be a monster.
Because monsters have to be made.

So they sent you to school
with the rest of the boys
like a calf to slaughter's blade.

It was they that changed you, wasn't it?
Told you how different you were and
showed you what cruelty looked like.

They called you abomination
as they struck you till you bled,
speared your sweetness with their word like spikes.

Ariadne your half-sister was the only one
other than your mother who loved you,
who understood you, who didn't fear your stature.

But as time wore on they took your kindness
and you began to see only cruelty
and blood wherever you saw youth gather.

Ariadne tried to make you see reason.
She tried to show you how to be good again
by showing you softness and the way to be human.

But there was no controlling your anger,
inside you the fury grew and grew
until you had given yourself to the demon.

So they built you a labyrinth and tossed you underground,
built a prison for a creature
and hoped you would die when you hit the ground.

But you lived through it.
Lived for the sickle moon of good inside you.
Lived because your sister still loved you.

Slowly, your heart died in the maze.
You became the nightmare everyone wanted you to be,
only Ariadne knew what you needed well.

When she sent Theseus to you,
she was sending you help.
It was easy for him to kill you,
for he was releasing you from hell.

(At least someone loved you enough to set you free.)

ATHENA'S GIFT TO MEDUSA

They portrayed her as evil,
turned her into a creature
when once she was a beautiful woman,
but she did not miss her beauty.

No, she asked Athena for this.
She traded her hair for snakes,
her soft green eyes for stone makers,
so no man would make her a tragedy,

Not the way Poseidon had done to her
when she was a priestess, just a girl.
This was her armor;
she would become a legend.

She would take on the form
of nightmares and terrify every man
who came looking to find
anything remotely human.

As long as they couldn't see the girl
that Poseidon nearly destroyed that
the demon armor protected,
she could stand fearless and tall.

She could become a myth,
a story to fear,
but never again
let anyone make her small.

A TINY STORY FOR ORPHEUS AND EURYDICE

The saddest word
in the whole wide world
is the word almost.

They were almost forever.
She was almost good for him.
He almost stopped her.
She almost waited.
He almost didn't look back.
She almost lived.
They almost made it.

HERA SHOWS US WHAT A TOXIC LOVE CAN DO TO YOU

Ask me why I became evil,
and I will take you back to Olympus with me and
show you the pain of being married to him,
show you the curse of being his lonely wife.

Not all of us wear our loneliness like it is a badge;
some of us bristle, some of us refuse its rags.
I am the Queen of the Gods but the daughter of Titans,
and they made me the protector of all married women.

But no one was there to protect me
or my heart when I needed it;
nothing but my anger, growing like a poison,
a hatred buried inside it.

What would you do if he filled your mouth
with wriggling worms of lies in every kiss?
And you couldn't hurt him because you loved him?
If he was both your curse and your bliss?

This is what the wrong love can do;
it slowly calcifies your heart from inside

till you feel nothing but the cold anymore.
It will make a villain out of you.

He stole my heart and turned it into stone
and expected me to just bear all of this.
Even as the queen of the gods, I was just a woman
he abandoned constantly yet still called his.

Was I cruel to those who deserved better?
Absolutely and I completely agree.
But tell me, what would you do
if you were me?

Would you handle his lies?
Be kind and be trampled over for eternity?
Or find an outlet for the anger,
devour everything he loved,

till in his heart there was
no more room for anything to be
till he recognized his greed was destroying them
till he could finally see only me,

only me,

only me.

ACHILLES BOY

You have been praying so long
for the strength to outlive the pain
they inflicted on you, that you have forgotten–
you are *already* strong.

That heart of yours was crafted
from the same clay as that of Achilles
last true warrior on the sands of Troy,
fighting a war that was a decade long.

Do you think Achilles wept
over the fates of lesser warriors
who tried and failed
to slaughter him?

Do you think you should lose sleep
over the lesser people
who tried to drown you in sorrow
and hoped you couldn't swim?

Listen to your heart, my brave soldier.
You have seen crueler battlefields than this.
If you were so resilient through them,
then you know, you *will* survive this.

THE FACE THAT LAUNCHED A THOUSAND SHIPS

I make no excuses for the ashes
nor the bones, but I do say this,
they told the world Paris stole me
but women are not objects to be stolen.

Make no mistake, I knew what I was doing.
After all, I was half-god,
and gods are arrogant.
We do not quake at ending mortals.

Here is a truth:
Gods and monsters are the same.

Here is another truth:
Your mothers tell you about
the monsters under your beds,
but they don't warn you
that sometimes

monsters come dressed as people
who claim to love you
more than the sun loves the moon,
with lies that fall from beautiful lips.

If anyone ever asks you if you knew
that monsters can be beautiful, too,
tell them about the face
that launched a thousand ships.

THE TWELVE LETTERS I SENT YOU TO REMIND YOU THAT YOU AREN'T HERCULES AND WE AREN'T MYTHOLOGY

1.

You were so torrentially toxic to me I had to slice my own veins to get you out.

2.

There was more chaos in the way you loved me than there was in the winding weather storm that broke every window in the house we called home; you turned that home into a house.

3.

You claimed momentary insanity, like your hero Hercules, the day you used your fists for the first time, the same insanity that plagued Hercules when he slew everyone he loved. I wonder if there was a storm where he lived that day, too.

4.

Harbinger made of hemlock and heartache, hurricane made of hurt and heartbreak, you were Hera's lesson of harm and habit, you were impossible to break, but I, too, like you, have hidden the strength of Hercules somewhere inside this harbor body that used to welcome hurricanes. I, too, have always known siren songs that have bewitched men with more ancient madness than you could ever imagine. I, too, have spoken words that dripped with cruelty like a soldier's sword in a battlefield, I do not use these abilities against you because I have learned, I have learned that when you destroy someone you love…there is no coming back from that.

5.

I was tied to my heartache the way Prometheus was tied to his mountain the day I met you. In my eyes, you were Hercules then. Freeing me from my destructive punishment, allowing me to finally breathe free. And like Prometheus, I, too forgot that Hercules was the son of the same God who punished him so cruelly. Our love became the new mountain I was tied to, the eagle forever circling, waiting for its moment to draw chunks from us again.

6.

There is no building from the wreckage of two broken hearts lying in the battlefields of an Olympus that will never be great or beautiful again. I wish you had seen that before I had to force you out of my blood by draining the poison you pumped into me during a war; poison I drank like it was the antidote to my war wounds.

7.

Do you think in the moment Hercules realized that he had killed everyone he loved, he chose to do those twelve tasks not as an apology but as a suicide mission?

8.

I'm drunk out of my mind, and I just wanted to say that you are no Hercules, there is no honor in the way your fingers threw me across the room with intent to harm. There was no madness in your eyes. Just hate.

9.

I'm sober as I can be and I just wanted to say you are no Hercules, because at least he grieved killing those he loved, whereas you didn't even feel sorry for shattering every part of me that you claimed to love.

10.

I love you and I hate myself for loving you.

11.

I hate you and I hate myself for hating you.

12.

On the day Hercules completed his twelfth task, he traveled to the sea. Sitting there on the cliffs, he saw the oncoming hurricane as it drank from the sea. He dove into the water, hoping…praying it would take his life with it. Instead, it delivered him back to the harbor where a man called Jason was just about to set sail for the golden fleece. And I learned that the gods did not want Hercules to die. Just like the gods did not want our love to live.

THE
WONDER

And if you asked
the sun what he
loved the most,
he would say
it was the darkness,
because it was what
helped him shine.

ELECTRICITY

You have enough electricity
inside you to power
a 40-watt lightbulb for 24 hours,
so why aren't the firefly-like embers
in your eyes glowing?
Are you really going to allow
someone to steal your ability
to light up your own life?

LESSONS FROM
A TINY NAVIGATOR

When I was a child afraid
of the night's intentions
someone I loved told me
it is full of strange and lovely truths
if you truly pay attention.

They told me about dung beetles
who use the Milky Way
to navigate their path like seafarers
of older days as they traveled
ancient oceans' dangerous lays.

And that on a clear night
if you are ever lost in the countryside
look up, and you can see

19,000,000,000,000,000 miles
into the exoskeleton map of the cosmos.

So even now, when my heart
is full of fear of the dark
I think of a tiny dung beetle
relying on a galaxy to find
its own way home.

And I reason if such
a tiny, easily forgotten being
can learn to see truth in the stars,
then who am I not to look up at them
in hope and read them with love till I am home?

HEALING LOOKS
SO DIFFERENT WITH YOU

You may be the loneliest thing
that I have ever loved.

I may be the most hurt thing
you have ever given your self to.

And some nights, talking does not make sense
for you are lost somewhere trying to find yourself

and I am still trying to recover in the quiet of afters.
After destruction, after violence, after trauma.

But on the nights we do talk,
we hold all the little hopes in this world to our chests

and turn them into healing.
Like the time I had a panic attack and couldn't breathe

until you told me about squirrels accidentally building
forests
because they constantly forgot where they put acorns.

Or the time you forgot how to speak for a week
until I held your hand and told you I will always be here

by telling you about how sea otters hold hands when they
sleep to stop themselves from drifting apart.

And you know our language probably sounds silly
to anyone else listening,

But this is better than the tequila
I once drowned myself in.

Or the people you got lost in when you were finding yourself.

And healing may look strange on us,
but I would rather be here, healing with you

than finding an escape
inside of somebody else.

THE THEORY OF YOU

If you do not consider yourself
a testament to the impossible
let me help you understand:
You are an assortment of seven octillion atoms,
carving out their very own fate
with stardust-powered hands.

ASK THE TREES

Ask the trees
and they will tell you
they have only existed
for a tenth
of Mother Earth's lifetime.
They will whisper to you
in wind-carried secrets,
that before them
mystical things existed here.

Even the oldest oak
is a young something to someone.
Even the most ancient cypress
once was a sapling.
Even you, though young now,
will become as wise and revered
the way they have if you allow
your growth to evolve you
as it evolved them little by little
every day.

There is a science to your survival.
There is a chemistry to your courage.
There is a physics to your power.
There is astronomy to your ancient.

Allow no one the opportunity
or the moment to take it away.

SIMPLE CHEMISTRY

An ounce of grace,
with a touch of humility
collected in a vial
made from clear remorse.

Heat this on acknowledgement
this potion made of sincerity
and finally, rely on your courage
to drink this,

the chemistry of an apology.

A NOTE ON TOGETHERNESS AFTER 2016

After "Collective Nouns For Humans In The Wild"
By Kathy Fish

Togetherness is nature's
only way to ensure
survival.

A collection of stars is called a constellation.
A cluster of constellations is called a galaxy.
A crowd of galaxies is called a supercluster.

A pandemonium of parrots.
A kettle of hawks.
A storytelling of ravens.

A pride of lions.
A sleuth of bears.
A band of coyotes.

But a group of humans
in their current state
of regression is called a damage.

A damage of humans.
A division of humans.
A destruction of humans.

THE MEANING OF FREEDOM

All of the wild things in nature
only know one kind of freedom.
That is the freedom of the soft earth
the freedom of the rain on their dense fur
the freedom of running where they please.
Yet if you talk to humans all we can talk about
is security, mundanity, and stability.
And still at night when our hearts
yearn for the moon we lie awake wondering
about how many different meanings freedom has
and is this truly what it means to be free?

HOW A STAR DIES

All this light
that travels so bravely
across the universe
to finally meet
with a human eye
and die there.

The star that sent its light to us
chose to die here,
in the arms of someone
made from parts
of the constellation
it once called its own.

LIMESTONE

Sometimes our feelings
about the ones who hurt us
that we still care for so deeply
are best described
as limestone.

Rarely formed pure
as they are marked with impurities.
In every single shade imaginable
influenced by our heart's wants
but also our uncertainties.

SURVIVAL OF THE KINDEST

When people speak of survival,
they will tell you about
"survival of the fittest."
What they don't know is
that Darwin also believed
in "survival of the kindest."

So when someone tries to tell you
that kindness is not strength,
that only the fittest will survive,
remind them that for Darwin,
the fittest humans were those
that help others thrive.

YOUR TRAUMA
DOES NOT DEFINE YOU

There is a reason why these dark memories haunt you every night. You see, the human brain has the capacity to store the equivalent of four terabytes. Four terabytes leaves a whole lot of room for terrible tragedies, but you must remember that you are stronger than your strife.

The things that hurt you, that caused you pain, do not define you. Nothing that broke you, that caused you the most intense damage, deserves the right to define who you are. They are things that happened to you, that evolved you as a person that changed you, but they still do not get the right to define your beautiful, brilliant soul which contains a tiny universe as vast as the one you see as endless in the night sky.

Did you know that just one human brain is able to generate more electrical impulses in a day than all the telephones in the world combined? And when such a powerful weapon falls into the hands of trauma, it uses it to manipulate you until it has chained you to itself, held your hope in a bind, molded you to its own definition.

Do not listen to it. It does not have the capacity to define the wonder that is you.

What does define you is your survival, your ability to have experienced awful things and still found it inside yourself to survive, to have the kind of courage so many would not dream of, to grow wings where yours had been taken and cut down.

You are made of beautiful, incredible, impossible things and your trauma does not get to trick you into believing that it is the only thing about you that matters.

Remember. You will shed your skin 1,000 times over your lifetime. The person who you were before damage came for you, that person is long gone and they will not be coming back, but remnants of them remain. Together the damage and the past before it have made you a brand-new human, a stronger human, a better human.

Remember that your bones are five times stronger than steel and you have forged yourself. From the very womb of your sadness, from the womb of your old self, you have come out, borne of heartache and pain. So no. After all that fighting you have done, your trauma does not get to define you, my dear heart.

Remember. Your heart is the size of a human fist, so you could take on your trauma in a bar fight and win. You are whole despite it. A better, braver, stronger you in every single way.

Your heart beats 104,000 times in a day and each one of those heartbeats is too valuable to waste thinking you are less than, just because your trauma tells you so. You were given your heart's unique rhythm to dance to, not to allow your trauma to speak over it so loud that you feel like you are going to drown.

THE
BEGINNING

First admit that you are unhappy.
Then admit why.
Then understand you need to let go.
Allow yourself a moment.
Breathe in the moment deeply.
Then the healing will begin.

CLASSIFICATION

I classify my books by genre.
Science fiction, romance, poetry.

I classify my people by emotion.
Who reminds me of stormy weather.
Who makes me do better.
And who helps me breathe.

A REFLECTION OF MY PARENTS:

I hear it all the time from other people:
"I hope I do not become my parents."

And whilst it is tempting to look
at my father and my mother and see their flaws,
for they are only human,
my heart now can only see
my father's kindness and generosity,
when he gives help to anyone
who asks without a single question,
my mother's fire and dignity
when someone pushes her too hard
and she gracefully puts them in their place.

I do not know if I will ever be like them.
But I hope I can do justice
to the people they are
by being the best person I can be someday.

RISE AND SHINE

Today is a good day
to rise from the darkness
where you have locked yourself
inside a body that
is more wound than home,
to greet the sun
who has been waiting
for this moment,
this splendid moment
for you to forgive yourself.

A SELF-PORTRAIT IN SELF-LOVE

What I said:

Love someone who is kinder to you
than you are to yourself.

What I meant:

You are in the business of being
your own worst nightmare.
If the world was ending
you would be the first
to sacrifice yourself
but not because you are trying
to do "the right thing,"
but because you want it all to end,
You find parts of yourself so repellent
you lay on the self-hatred like it is perfume
to cover up the stink of absolute despair
wholeheartedly agree with your critics,
become the worst of your own bullies,
intimidate those who hate you
with how much you hate yourself.
You are the sort of human being
who has become an urgent cry for help,
for a person to step in
and humanize you in your own eyes
by being kind to you
so you can learn to love yourself.

MORE TRUTHS ABOUT YOU

Stop pretending
to be a cry
in the dark.

You are a morning
waiting to happen
to someone.

HOW A LAMB
REJECTS THE SLAUGHER

What I Wrote Post-Survival When I Was 14:

Some girls are full of heartache and poetry
and those are the girls who try to save wolves
instead of running away from them.

What I meant:

The first step is when someone points out a behavior as
abusive which you have normalized in your own head.

The second step is when you Google
"am I being emotionally abused?"

The third step is realizing that if you have to Google "am I
being emotionally abused?," it usually means you are.

The fourth step is realizing that you have turned your mind
into a place where wolves like to hunt you and silly girl,

you keep running back to them to save them, don't you? Listen to their apologies from bloodied fangs that have been feasting on your self-worth and buy them like a lamb, hoping that they still love you because you still believe in the fairy tale of love. The idea that if someone truly loves you, they will never ever hurt you, whereas it is the people who claim to love you the most that hurt you the most.

Step five will be taking this forest mind of yours and remembering why you never trust a wolf. Do not let him apologize. Do not allow him to guilt you into an apology. Do not swallow your pride for him or let him addle your mind. You are a girl, not a lamb to the slaughter. And if there is one thing girls know how to do, it is survive.

The final step:
End his control over you.
Then turn your back on him
and run.

THE ONLY RULE ABOUT LIVING

Everything we love
and everything we know,
all of living is encapsulated
in a single act,
the act of letting go.

THE TRUTH ABOUT
LIFE AND SUFFERING

They say, "Yes, you will suffer."

But they don't say, "But you will also experience the deepest of joys. You will experience the births and deaths of the greatest of loves. You will grow and gain beautiful lessons about your own humanity along the way. You will experience the seasons in all of their incredible glory. And the ocean at your feet on a hot summer's day, the sand tickling your skin as you walk away from it. And the sun warming the blood under your skin after the coldest of winter. And the rain against your window will sing you to a peaceful sleep. And you will awaken some mornings in the arms of someone who will love you most of all. And experience the highest of achievements as a human. You may hold a son or a daughter or a baby brother or a sister or a niece, and realize how precious life is. You will feel your parents' love for the first time sometimes and understand how much they love you. There will be moments where you are broken, true. But there will also be moments when your soul will gleam so beautifully, even the universe will bask in your happiness. Yes, you will suffer. But you will be happy beyond your wildest dreams. And that will make every second of the suffering worth it."

They should say that, all of that. Because it is that balance that makes us beautifully and softly human.

And that, that is the greatest gift that we have been given.

HOW TO BE STRONG:

There are no rules.
You are already strong.

Even when you are feeling yourself falling apart
in the most public place you know.

Even when your knees hit the floor
and your grief meets you in floods.

Even when your body wracks with sobs
Crafted in the belly of a tsunami.

Even when sorrow feels like
an endless drowning.

Your fortitude is right there,
inside you.

Your strength is within you always
to call up when you want to.

And besides, didn't anyone ever tell you
that survival, that resilience,

that strength looks
so different on us all?

On some it look like still waters and on others
it looks like a dam bursting as the water falls.

A REMINDER
AS WE REACH THE END

To love yourself
should be no quiet affair,
but a loud uprising.

RAB RAKHA

In Punjabi,
my native tongue,
we do not say
goodbye.

Instead, we say
"Rab rakha"
which loosely translated means
"God be with you."

And this incantation
of protection
is so much more drenched with love
than a simple goodbye.

So to you I say,
"Rab rakha."
May God always be with you
on this long journey, on your way.

FROM WRITER TO READER

Allow me to tell you
what a privilege it has been
to have been been
created from the same dust,
droplets of cosmic rain,
ancient energy
and cradled
by our Mother Universe,
in the same
interstellar nursery
as you.

WITH DEEPEST GRATITUDE TO:

Bianca and Chris,
for their infinite patience,
their kindness,
their honesty.

Steve
for his strength
and his fortitude.

Amanda, Trista, Caitlyn, Rob,
Clare, Layla, Ross,
Tristan, Joanna,
Emma, Lauz,
for their friendship.

My family
for understanding
the path I have chosen
and their support.

And you.
For giving a home
to the words.
Thank you.

ABOUT THE AUTHOR

Nikita Gill lives just outside a forest in England.
She's a writer, photographer, and graphic designer.
She loves the night sky.

Find her on:
facebook.com/nikitagillwrites
instagram.com/nikita_gill